Writing Brave Press
1940 Palmer Avenue, #1032
Larchmont NY 10538
www.writingbravepress.com

Distributed by IngramSpark

Cover and Text Design: Karinna Klocko
Copyeditor: Meghan Muldowney
Author Photos: Heike Martin with Heike Martin Photography

Library of Congress Cataloging-in-Publication Data available.
ISBN 979-8-9873704-7-6 (Paperback)
ISBN 979-8-9873704-8-3 (eBook)

First Edition

Foreword

I heard Megan's voice when I picked up my cell phone.
"I can hardly say these words, but my mother just died."
I was stunned. How could this be. Her mother was fine.
I noticed the impulse to ask questions, to know the details.
The vigilance center in my brain leaped toward information
as if I were in danger and getting the facts will remind me
I am safe. I noticed my impulse and put it on pause. I took
long breath, "Be with her" an inner voice guided me.
"Just be the safe holding space for her."

Neither of us could have imagined the next months. The
sudden decline of her father and his death which thrust
Megan into the role no one wants — a complex estate
process with her name as executrix.

Megan has always been a curious, insightful, and
compassionate person. She thinks systemically and can
connect dots in ways that organize pathways to healing.
I saw this in her when she first walked into my classroom
and as I supervised her training to be a therapist. In this
workbook, she offers you that gift. Across the many months
of grief and executrix work, Megan engaged faithfully the
complicated functions of the estate process. And, she
created protected spaces to notice, tend, and work through
her layered losses.

Always a woman of hope and resilience, Megan noticed the severe gaps in the resources for persons who are simultaneously bearing the impact of personal losses while navigating a cumbersome estate system that all too often misses the person, documents in hand, standing before them. Her attentiveness to her personal journey, and attunement to what could be different birthed this workbook in your hands.

Megan's skills as educator, pastor, and therapist are intertwined in her lovely presentation to you the reader. You are provided a rich array of resources to guide and support you if you are walking this journey. Megan skillfully weaves sample forms and scripts as well as to do lists and charts to helpfully track each step along the way. All of this paired with care for yourself and what you need in this massive reorientation process of grief and estate settlement.

I wish you wellness on your journey.

— *Janet Stauffer, PhD, Kairos University*

*For my parents, Guy and Rebecca Malick, who
taught me how to love with my whole heart and
to share what I have learned with others.*

A NEW PATH

A Practical Workbook and Planner for the First Year of Grief and Settling Your Person's Affairs

By Megan Malick

Hello Fellow Griever

I invite you to pause for a moment. Imagine we sit across from one another. I offer you a cool glass of water or a warm cup of tea. We look at one another eye to eye. I hold your gaze in mine. I send you love and compassion to support you in this moment of pause.

I hesitate to say the word welcome. Most folks don't desire to be here or to read these pages. We meet because someone you love died or is terminally ill. In addition to your grief, you face the task of resolving the logistical affairs of their life. Whether you are the legally appointed representative, executor, or not, this book seeks to companion you through the next year.

Did you presume the paperwork and practical tasks of loss should not be emotional? Have you found yourself upset or triggered by mundane chores? If that's true, it makes complete sense! In my experience, each piece of paper filed and resolved felt like letting go of my people a little bit more. The practical aspects of paperwork and property enflesh the absence of your person.

For the spiritual but not necessarily religious, I invite you to see the journey as sacred. As you mourn and face the to-do lists, you are indeed walking in the thin spaces between life and death.

Our Work Together could be considered **The Tasks of Mourning.**

Grief counselor William Worden encourages the bereaved to engage with their grief through tasks of mourning:

- **Task I:** To accept the reality of the loss
- **Task II:** To process the pain of grief
- **Task III:** To adjust to a world without the deceased
- **Task IV:** To find an enduring connection with the deceased in the midst of embarking on a new life

Our culture's deadlines and pressures push you through so much so quickly. The tasks of mourning are pillars to remind you of all the emotional and spiritual labor that are part of settling your person's affairs.

For the purpose of this journal, your grief and the physical process of estate settling become a way to move through the tasks of mourning. Each to-do on your list holds the emotional labor of mourning–of recognizing the loss and integrating it.

That's right. Each to-do on your list represents so much more than a task. Each piece of paper symbolizes your person. It feels like a lot sometimes because it is. And there are people and places to turn to that will support you on this journey.

With you on the journey,

M.M.

Megan
AKA The Accidental Matriarch

A Brief Note

Please know that all of the practices and ideas are invitations for you. They are not 'musts' or 'shoulds' or 'have tos.' I know you will have many of those. So if you come to a page or a practice that is not for you, simply let it go.

As someone who reads for pleasure and writes to make meaning in my world, my loss of language felt so fierce in the early days of grief. The suggestions I received from others to write led to this poem:

Missing Words

In the early days
Words would come and go as randomly as...
There

they went just now while typing

This happened consistently and comprehensively
in those early days.

I audio messaged and emailed with friends
Trying to tether myself to this world
This reality
This moment.

They encouraged me to write more and promised
writing would steady me

But I just couldn't in those early days
Too much
Too heavy
Too overwhelming

No Words left

I had me and silence.

If you find yourself speechless and silent, please know you are not alone.

TABLE OF CONTENTS

This planner/workbook serves as a guidebook for your journey. Like geographical guidebooks, it can't and won't detail your unique and specific journey. It provides an overview. The book is organized in sections:

1 Grief and How to Live With and in Grief

- **Information about grief, grieving, and the brain**
- **Practices to help you be with yourself and ask for help**
- **Basic Needs**

2 Helpers and Asking for Help

- Places to list and organize your support people
  - *Your Trees:* family and friends who can support you physically, mentally, emotionally, and spiritually. You will see charts and graphic organizers for you to identify your trees and list their contact information.
  - *Your Forest Rangers:* professionals like your estate attorney, financial advisor, realtor, accountant, after loss professional, whom you hire for their specific expertise.
- Sample text or email messages to ask for help from your trees

3 Logistics

- Rituals for honoring the Sacred in the journey
  - Ritual for Opening and Closing Sacred Space
  - Ritual for Releasing
  - Creating Your Own Ritual
- Lists of the Tasks of Settling Your Person's Affairs

4 Monthly and Weekly Organizer and Planner

- Monthly Organizers
- How To Use the Weekly Planner
- Weekly Planner and Reflection
- Monthly Reflection

5 More Practices and Education about Grief

- Just for Today: practice to support you daily
- Practices to Support Yourself in Stress and Bereavement
- Education about Dual Roles and their connection to stress
- Education about Chronic Stressors and Ways to Support Yourself in Chronic Stress
- Education and Reflection about Secondary Losses

6 Resources for Settling Your Person's Affairs

- Glossary of Terms
- Summary of the Difference between Estate and Probate
- Tools Available to Help You Stay Organized
- Sample Death Notification Letter to Utility Companies and State Agencies
- Sample Death Notification Letter to Financial Institutions
- Sample Chart/Spreadsheet for Tracking Debts and Assets
- Sample Form for Tracking Bank
- Sample Script for Talking with Financial Institutions
- Sample Form for Tracking Investment Accounts
- Sample Chart for Beneficiary Contact Information

Disclaimer for your Journey

Every part of this should be considered an option. Every person is unique. Every grief is unique. The estate process for each loss is unique. Some parts may not be applicable to grief and your situation.

Hopes and Dreams Railway

Pocket of Peace

Chapter 1: Grief and How to Live With and in Grief

If you find yourself struggling with things that used to be easy...
If you struggle to remember things or keep track of small details...
If you recognize that you feel irritated, frustrated, sad, or exhausted easily and often...
Your brain is having a normal reaction to grief.

Here are some common symptoms of acute grief. **Mark the ones you experience.**

- ☒ Brain fog
- ○ Difficulty sleeping
- ○ Difficulty concentrating
- ○ Intense moods
- ○ Dramatic mood changes over "little things"
- ○ Exhaustion and fatigue
- ○ Anger and potentially rage
- ○ Expecting to see or hear your person
- ○ Thinking you did see or hear your person
- ○ Numbness
- ○ Change in appetite

This phase is often the worst during the first 6 months.

Space to reflect

What's going on with my brain?

- As mammals, our brains seek close people — our attachments — and when we're with them, we feel comfort.

- Brains in grief seek our close person.

- When we don't find them, the felt sense lights up inside.

- The neural pathway of seeking and not finding leads to panic and then, without comfort, leads to rage and fear.

- This whole cycle activates our stress hormones, so grief is just as much physiological as it is emotional.

The Double Whammy of Stressors

Your brain is trying to make sense of the unsensible – your person is no longer physically here. The networks in your brain that hold the memory, emotion, and the physical space memories of your person ALL have to re-learn that your person is not physically here.

As you are in this new world of settling someone's logistical affairs, you also need to learn that new world while also learning to live in this world without them.
It's a double whammy.

That's right. It isn't fair or right that just as your brain, body, and spirit are suffering this loss, you are also entering into this new terrain where the road map can seem to be written in a different language.

The Dual Process Model of Bereavement

Stroebe and Schut developed the Dual Process Model. Grievers travel back and forth from loss orientation to restoration orientation. Stressors can be part of both experiences. The sphere outside represents "everyday life."

Loss / Grief

Thinking about death
Big emotions
Rumination
Avoiding moving forward, making decisions
Reflecting on your secondary losses
Processing grief with journal, art, talking, crying

Restoration / Rebuilding

Attending to life changes
Learning new things
Doing new things
Redefining role identity
Cultivating new relationships
Distracting from grief loss

Adapted from Stroebe and Schut, 2001

If you need a quick reminder:

- When you feel overwhelmed, or frustrated, I invite you to pause and consider the Olympian mental, emotional, spiritual, and physical work you are doing.

- Your body and brain are grieving.

- Grief makes ALL brains and bodies stressed out.

- Grief doesn't just go away in a week, month, a year. You learn to live with grief rather than it resolving (and you will learn to carry it).

- Grief comes in waves and can feel "out of the blue."

- Settling someone's affairs is stressful WITHOUT grief.

- The system is not built for grieving bodies/brains.

- You're in a double whammy. You're stressed and that makes sense.

BASIC NEEDS

When we're in grief, life can be confusing, disorienting, and overwhelming. There are so many demands placed upon grievers on top of the emotional wound of your loss.

For many of us, it's helpful to have reminders for **what helps us survive.**

I invite you to see meeting your basic needs as one of the ways you can care for yourself on your bereavement pilgrimage. Meeting your basic needs can help sustain you when the day is long and the climb is steep. These are suggestions and invitations for you to adapt to meet your unique grief journey, as is everything in this book,.

Mark or make notes besides the **BASIC NEEDS** that you find most supportive and helpful. Put an ** next to the **BASIC NEEDS** you want to add. When grief and the logistical work feel overwhelming and consuming, return to your **BASIC NEEDS.**

Breathe — Sometimes when we're stressed, overwhelmed, or in grief, we hold our breath. Take a moment and just allow your breath to flow.

Activity — Movement and physical activity can help our nervous systems to discharge extra energy and help us to ground. Any daily movement is good: walking, yoga, jogging, biking, swimming, dancing, weightlifting, kickboxing.

Sleep — Sleep can be difficult early in bereavement. Try to lie down and rest each night if you're struggling to sleep.

Identifying — Your Emotions: Early grief is like an ocean of mixed emotions, and the waves can be large. Taking time to name your emotions and possibly journaling about them or recording them in a voice recorder can help you to process and release the emotions.

Clean — Bathe or shower daily. Taking time to stand in the shower allowing the water to wash over you, soaking in the tub, or simply washing your face daily can help your body feel some renewal.

Nature
Take time to get outside a little each day. Sunlight and fresh air can help your body to feel nourished. The Vitamin D from the sun can also help restore you.

Eat
Eat every day. Try to eat some protein, fresh fruits, and vegetables in regular intervals. Even if it's just a few bites. If smoothies are easier, start there.

Explore
Check out books, music, movies, TV shows, podcasts, and other forms of entertainment that can help take your mind from your grief. If reading is too much, try an audio book. If a movie is too long, stream a TV show.

Drink
Water: Try to drink 6-8 glasses of water daily. If that's too much, sip water throughout the day.

Stop
When a grief burst comes, see if you can stop what you're doing to allow it to rise, crest, and fall like a wave. If you're driving a car, pull over. If you're at work, excuse yourself and go to the bathroom.

Write down 3-5 BASIC NEEDS that you commit to practicing.

1.

2.

3.

4.

5.

Chapter 2: Helpers & Asking for Help

Who are the Trees Nourishing and Sheltering You Through Your Grief Journey?

1. Write a list of people who offered to help. You can look at your text messages, emails, and social media threads to help generate your list.

_____   _____

_____   _____

_____   _____

_____   _____

_____   _____

_____   _____

2. Like the diversity of the trees in the forest, our friends and family all have different gifts. Some people can be with us through it all; they can lend a hand, an ear, a shoulder, and a distraction. Some people help us organize and do tasks. Other people are our emotional support, while others help us to rediscover the joy in life. Look at the 2 charts below and go back to your list of friends and family, and consider the kind of tree each person is for you.

Friend / Family Name	Contact Information	Type of Tree

Type of Tree	Description	Support Strength Areas
Redwood	Support friend or family who has love and energy to give. They can be with you when you're sad. They can help you get shit done. They know you well and can pivot easily.	• Helping you fill out this planner • Touching base with you daily • Sharing with you as you tell stories, remembering the past, and honoring your boundaries when set • Going with you to meet with the pastor, the attorney, the financial advisor • Sitting with you while you cry AND helping you with your to-do list at the same time • Going through belongings with you if you're having trouble deciding what to keep, donate, and dispose
Oak Trees	Support friend or family who is organized and is a "do-er." They may not give you a shoulder to cry on, but they are comfortable rolling up their sleeves and jumping in.	• Organizing people for meals, luncheons, and other needs • Creating phone/email trees to send messages out; they become the switch board so you don't have to • Helping you pack up belongings and donations • Taking charge of cleanout once you're ready for that • Calling around to places to find out information • Doing your household tasks: laundry, dog walking, cat litter scooping, meal making, cleaning
Weeping Willow	No emotion is off limit for these friends. They do not shy away from the feral nature of grief. They can weep with you and rage with you. They are comfortable witnessing emotions without trying to fix or solve them.	• Providing support after you've heard a song, had a memory, or any other grief activator, and when you feel alone and sad • Coming over to be with you on a sad day and letting you simply be as you are • Giving hugs and holding you while you cry
Fruit Trees	These support people are wonderful for helping you set your grief aside for a moment and savor some of the joys in life. They are good at helping distract with outings and activities.	• Coming with you to the movies, to explore a small town, or to take a hike in the woods • Planning small outings for you

Your Professional Guides
AKA Your Forest Rangers

Type of Forest Ranger	Names/Contact Information	Description	Check the Rangers you need
Elder Care Attorney		Provides support to elderly clients and their families both before & after death, can provide guidance & support to the executor/ administrator through the probate process	
Estate Attorney		Helps with the probate process and guides the executor/administrator through the probate process & estate administration process.	
Paralegal		Works under the supervision of the attorney to provide support through probate process.	
Financial Advisor		Reviews financial documents, identifies beneficiaries, and advises executor in asset value, possible asset liquidation, & asset distribution. Collaborates and consults with attorney & accountant	
Estate Accountant or Tax Advisor		Assists with/completes tax forms as needed, advises on the tax implications for liquidating assets. May provide financial reports to beneficiaries. Collaborates and consults with attorney & financial advisor	

Type of Forest Ranger	Names/Contact Information	Description	Check the Rangers you need
Appraiser		Determines financial value of personal property, real estate, & businesses. Provides unbiased value of property within the estate.	
Real Estate Agent		Assists with preparing property to sell, streamlines the process, and provides alternatives for selling	
After Loss Professional		Provides one-on-one customized support/ guidance through the process of settling your person's affairs. Assists with planning logistics & administration by looking at all the pieces, and provides practical & emotional support.	
Professional Mediator		Facilitates conversations between stakeholders in estate process. Assists with identifying mutually agreeable solutions and navigating difficult decisions & complex situations.	
Family Therapist		Supports families emotionally and interpersonally, while they move through the grief & estate settling process, facilitates communication between family members	

What do you need?

One of the daunting tasks for many people early in grief is difficulty organizing thoughts, as well as knowing what they need. These sample messages can be photographed and texted to family or friends who ask, what do you need?

If you're struggling to let someone know what you need, see if one of these examples works. Take a picture and text it, copy it, or edit for your specific need.

Thank you so much for offering to help. I need help with arranging the funeral meal. Could you help me with that?

Thank you so much for offering to help. I could use meals. It's easiest for our family if you send gift cards through GrubHub, DoorDash, UberEATS.

Thank you so much for offering to help. Your ability to coordinate things would be great. Would you be willing to coordinate a meal train for our family for the next couple of weeks?

Thank you so much for offering to help. You are so good at seeing the little things. Would you be able to arrive at the funeral early and stay around to help make sure the little details are caught? Could you help bring things to and from places?

Thank you so much for offering to help. Would you be able to walk and feed the dog ——————————*?*
(date/time)

Thank you so much for offering to help. Would you be able to feed the cat and scoop litter ——————————*?*
(date/time)

Thank you so much for offering to help. Would you be able to take care of our pets on ——————————— *?*
(date/time)

Thank you so much for offering to help. You are so good at housekeeping. Would you be able to help with laundry and housecleaning?

Thank you so much for offering to help. Will you help me sort through the mail and pay bills?

Thank you so much for offering to help. I could use some help creating my to-do list for this week. Would you help me prioritize my week?

Thank you so much for offering to help. You are so good at cleaning out and organizing. We'd like to have a couple of work weekends. Would you be willing to help us coordinate and plan a clean out work weekend?

Chapter 3: Logistics

Ritual for Opening and Closing Sacred Space of Logistics Work

Preparing Your Sacred Space

If it is right for you and your body, find a space in your home that you can dedicate to working on your person's paperwork.

Perhaps adorn your working area with plants, flowers, candles, or rocks.

Perhaps find framed photos of your person to place in your workspace.

Perhaps create an altar where you can honor your loved one and place objects of meaning.

All of the above are suggestions meant to resource you. Creating a visual and tangible symbol can be a way of feeling the support around you. It can be a spot to focus your eyes when you seek visual resourcing.

Beginning Logistical or Estate Work

Enter your adorned space to work. Adapt or adopt my ritual, or create a simple ritual of your own.

My Ritual

- Pause and allow your eyes to gaze at your altar and/or photos/objects.

- Breathe in and out for 2-3 breaths. Allow your feet to feel the floor.

My Ritual (cont.)

- Light one candle in honor of your departed beloved and any/all of your deceased loved ones who are with you and supporting you on this grief journey.

- Light the other candle for yourself and all those who physically support you.

- Place one hand on your heart and one on your stomach as you breathe slowly while gazing at the candles.

- If it is right for you, you can invoke Source/God/ Love/Higher Power/Universe to be with you today and through this time. You may also offer gratitude to your loved ones and to Source for their presence and support.

Write your intention for your work time on an index card or a sticky note. Place your written note on your altar or next to your candles/person's photo.
For example:

Today, I intend to call the home insurance company to make sure they received the death notification letter. I will also ensure that the policy has been transferred to _____'s name. I will ask what next steps are and record what I learn in the planner.

Once you have written your intention and placed it in your sacred space, offer a blessing or prayer for your time.

Divine Beloved,

Please be with me today as I work on the logistical work for my _____ . Help me to discern when to dig in and when to step away. Give me the endurance and patience I need today. When the grief swells, support and comfort me. When I want to quit, remind me that this paperwork is a task of mourning. That this work is sacred work.

I ask all of this in your many names.

Ending Logistical/Estate Work for the Day/Time

- Use the planner or your method of tracking your work to write yourself a few notes about where you're ending and what you want to pick up or return to next time you engage this work.

- Review the intention you set and credit yourself for showing up.

- Put papers away or close files.

- Envision closing and containing all the unanswered questions and concerns until you return. Everything will be here waiting for you.

- Take a few moments to notice your breath. Don't try to make it be any different. Simply notice it.

- If it's right for you and your body, notice the sensation of your feet touching the floor. Allow yourself to feel how gravity supports your body.

- Take a moment and turn your head slowly to the left and then to the right.

- Notice anything in your space that brings you a sense of comfort or support.

If it is helpful, say aloud,

I am _____ and I am in _____
          (your name)   *(where you are)*
_____ . I am _____ years old.

It is safe for me to stop this work for today.

End with a closing blessing/prayer.

Divine Beloved,

Thank you so much for supporting me today and watching over me. Please free me from any burden that I carry from this work today.

Support me as I shift from this work to
_____ .
(whatever you are doing next).

I ask this in your many names.

Blow out the candles. If you like, you may wash your hands, take a quick walk, or shake your body as a symbol of ending your work for this time.

Ritual for Releasing

As you settle your person's physical affairs, you feel grief. In a sense, each time you give some of their clothes away or close an account, you release their physical presence a little more.

A releasing ritual is to provide you space to honor this process.

Enter/Open Sacred Space

- Go to the altar/space you created to honor the life and legacy of your person.

- Pause and allow your eyes to gaze at your altar and/or photos/objects.

- Breathe in and out for 2-3 breaths. Allow your feet to feel the floor.

- Light one candle in honor of your departed beloved and any/all of your deceased loved ones who are with you and supporting you on this grief journey.

- Light the other candle for yourself and all those who physically support you.

- Place one hand on your heart and one on your stomach as you breathe slowly while gazing at the candles.

- If it is right for you, you can invoke Source/God/Love/ Higher Power/Universe to be with you.

Ritual of Release

- Say aloud, write, or think about what you released (or are about to release).

- Imagine holding it in your hands.

- If it is right for you and your body, offer thanks and gratitude for what you release.

- Imagine the hands of Source/Higher Power/the Divine beneath yours; they are ready to catch what you release.

- When you are ready, open your hands and imagine that you release this physical aspect of your person into the hands of Source/Higher Power/the Divine.

- If you like, sing a song, say a chant, or move your body as a means of support.

- If you like, spend a few moments with your journal to reflect on what you released.

Closing Sacred Space

Source of Love,

Bless me and _____
            (whatever you release).

Though this represents the physical end, open me to feel the support and presence that continue beyond this realm. Free me from any burdens or obligations that are not mine to carry. Comfort and guide me as I continue to this new path.

I ask this in your many names.

Blow out the candles. If you like, you may wash your hands, take a quick walk, or shake your body as a symbol of ending your work for this time.

Creating Your Own Ritual

What sets a ritual apart from a tradition?

Rituals are like living poetry. They make a change come alive by honoring that change. Real change affects more than just what we do. A real change takes body, mind, and spirit. Rituals also allow for the paradoxes and polarities to be seen, felt, named, and honored rather than resolved or reconciled.

How can I get started?

- Start with asking yourself some questions: What change or transition do you want to honor? What invisible spaces or places do your heart and soul see? How could highlighting these spaces and places support you? Spend some time journaling or verbally recording your thoughts. Perhaps invite one of your trees to be with you for this practice.

- What is the intention for your ritual? Protection, guidance, blessing, releasing, gratitude, something else, a combination of these...

- What elements in your life support you with remembering and connecting with Something Larger (Source/Higher Power/Divine/Spirit/Love)? Are there songs, movements, scents, images, or words that bring you a sense of meaning and comfort? Make a list in your journal or on the next page.

- Are there natural elements that would support you in this ritual: water, fire, rocks, or crystals? Make a list.

- Think about or map out a flow.
  - Opening
  - Ritual
  - Closing

- Collect your materials and practice. There is no right way... a ritual is to be supportive of you and your unique journey.

Creating Your Own Ritual

I want to honor the change and transition with...

The intention for this ritual is...

The language that feels most supportive to me is...

I would like to include these elements in my ritual...

The opening will be...

The ritual will be...

The closing will be...

Space to reflect

Tasks your forest rangers may guide or share with you	Tasks that trees can support, help, or take care of for you	Tasks that may require your presence but a tree could shelter and support you

Estate To-Dos
The Beginning of the Journey

First Things First

☒ Work with funeral home, hospice, faith community, and/or death doula for caring for your person's body, writing an obituary, planning/having a service, and creating payment agreement for funeral home services.

○ Arrange for care of children, elders, animals.

○ Secure the house/apartment.

○ Notify close friends and family.

○ Obtain death certificate.

○ Notify Social Security.

Find Important Documents

Find important documents:

○ Will, trust, legal documents, driver's license, Social Security card

○ Car title and registration

○ Deed to house

○ Mortgage

○ Insurance policy information

○ Bank name and account #s

Find Important Documents (cont.)

○ Investment and retirement account information and possibly financial planner information

○ Search email and online accounts for access to statements.

○ Contact student loan provider to report death and inquire about next steps.

Meet and hire an estate attorney to review probate process in your state

○ Review the will or trust with the estate attorney. Don't hesitate to ask questions if you don't understand something.

○ With your estate attorney, determine the process in your state for notifying beneficiaries/giving them access to the will/initiating probate.

○ Discuss assets and debts to determine a way to keep track of all assets and all debts.

○ Learn if you will need to pay inheritance tax, how that works, and what assets are included in that.

○ If there are laws about digital accounts and assets, ask what you need to do.

○ Open an estate bank account.

○ Obtain a Federal Tax Identification Number or an EIN (Employer Identification Number).

○ Wait to access safe deposit box, close bank account, or give away your person's belongings until you have a clear plan with your estate attorney or elder law attorney. **States have specific and different laws about this.**

Property/House Needs

Notify all companies of the death and get accounts transferred to the estate to pay.

Property/House Needs (cont.)

O Maintain property, which could include:

    O Lawn maintenance

    O Cleaning

    O Ensuring utilities are working and paid

O Pay bills out of estate bank account once that account has been opened.

O Forward the mail.

O Keep records of all bills and payments.

Death Notification

O If your person was employed, notify their employer. Talk with HR about next steps.

O Make a list of all credit card accounts and subscriptions.

    O Close accounts.

    O Send death notification letter and death certificate if needed.

O Contact Social Security to report death and learn about potential benefits and next steps in the process (1-800-325-0778).

O Contact student loan provider to report death and inquire about next steps.

O Contact the Veteran's Administration (VA) if your person was a veteran. Learn about potential supports and benefits you may receive.

O Run a credit check for your person, and notify all three of the big credit agencies (TransUnion, Equifax, and Experian) that your person is deceased.

O Ask for your person's credit report to be flagged as "Deceased: Do Not Issue Credit."

Death Notification (cont.)

O Once estate bank account is open, begin closing all other financial accounts and moving liquid assets to bank account for distribution.

O If beneficiaries are listed on accounts, the institution can help you begin moving those accounts.

O The process for death notification and account closing/ moving of assets varies from company to company, so taking notes, getting the phone number or contact information, and using the planner for follow up can be helpful.

In the Middle of the Journey

Planning and Working with your Professional Team

O Work with your estate attorney, financial advisor, or accountant to get a projection of the estate's cash flow.

  O Determine what debt must be paid.

  O Develop plan for liquidating assets in order to pay debt.

O Work with your estate attorney, financial advisor, or accountant to determine the best plan for moving and distributing assets.

O Work with your estate attorney for transferring any assets pertaining to intellectual property or copyright. You may need to work with an intellectual property lawyer.

O Clarify with your professional team what they do and what you need to do.

O Get tangible property assessed, such as real estate and jewelry.

Property/House Needs

○ Maintain property, which could include:

   ○ Lawn maintenance

   ○ Cleaning

   ○ Ensuring utilities are working and paid

○ Pay bills out of estate bank account once that account has been opened.

○ Cancel any unnecessary services or memberships.

○ Cancel cell phone.

○ Ensure that the executor/administrator's name is on the insurance policy.

○ Consider getting a security system if home is unoccupied.

○ Make decision about length of maintaining ownership or lease.

○ Begin packing, donating, and giving away items.

○ Keep records of all bills and payments.

Continue Death Notifications

○ Utilize record keeping system for documenting death notifications sent and any instructions you receive.

○ Contact student loan provider to report death and inquire about next steps.

Record Keeping System for Your Person's Things (Assets, Debts)

○ Create an inventory of real physical and personal property.

○ Create an inventory of non-probate assets.

Record Keeping System for Your Person's Things (Assets, Debts) (cont.)

O Create a financial record, running ledger, spreadsheet, or other method of listing the value of each asset. 🌲 🚶 🏞️

O Create a running ledger, spreadsheet, or other method for listing each debt. 🌲 🚶 🏞️

O Begin entering data into your record keeping systems. 🌲 🚶 🏞️

O Utilize credit report, bank account statements, and your person's email (if you have access to it) to find account information. 🌲 🚶 🏞️

O Share records with your estate attorney, financial advisor, and/or tax professional to develop a plan for liquidating, selling, and moving assets. 🚶

Consider what and how to share with beneficiaries (in consultation with an attorney).

O Possibly invite beneficiaries to assist with some of the tasks. 🚶

O Possibly hold meeting to share "State of the Estate" with beneficiaries. 🚶

O Possibly enlist help of after loss professional or financial family therapist to assist in deciding what to share with beneficiaries and how to share. 🚶

Moving Toward the End of the Process

Planning and Working with your Professional Team

O Meet with professional team to create plan for taxes and money needed to pay final debts. 🏃

O Collaborate with team to liquidate, transfer, and sell assets. 🏃

O Collaborate with team with how to communicate plan with beneficiaries. 🏃

O Consult with estate attorney about the estate's responsibility with outstanding debts. 🏃

Property/House Needs

O Maintain property, which could include: 🌳

   O Lawn maintenance

   O Cleaning

   O Ensuring utilities are working and paid

O If selling property:

   O Prepare for sale. 🌳

   O Work with realtor to list and sell real estate. 🏃

O Distribute, donate, or dispose of personal property and non-real estate personal assets.

O If keeping home or car, transfer titles. 🌳

O Consider an estate sale for the remaining items in the home. 🏃

Record Keeping System for Your Person's Things (Assets, Debts)

O Track expenses with receipts.

O Gather documents and data for final income tax return for your person. 🌳

O Communicate with creditors to ensure that any outstanding debts that the estate owes are paid. 🚶

Communications with Beneficiaries

O Share timeline about asset transfer and real estate property sale with beneficiaries.

O Distribute tangible property to beneficiaries.

O Contact student loan provider to report death and inquire about next steps. 🚶

At The End of the Process

Planning and Working with your Professional Team

O Collaborate with your professional team to distribute assets to beneficiaries. 🚶

O Consult with your team to see if you need to file an estate income tax return (Form 1041) for the estate. If so, work with them to file this return. 🚶

O Collaborate with your professional team to compile a final accounting of the estate's assets, liabilities, and distributions. 🚶

O Request estate attorney provide a release from liability to give to beneficiaries. 🚶

O Complete steps necessary to close the estate in your specific location. Consult with your attorney for these steps. 🚶

Property/House Needs

O Ensure that any remaining personal property not specifically mentioned in the will is distributed appropriately. 🌳

O Mail:

  O File two Change of Address forms from post office. 🌳

  O Fill out one form from your person's previous residence and under "New Mailing Address," write Deceased. 🌳

  O Fill out the second form for the address that currently receives your person's mail. 🌳

  O Under "New Mailing Address," write Deceased. 🌳

Record Keeping System for Your Person's Things (Assets, Debts)

O Confirm that all outstanding debts, taxes, and expenses of the estate have been settled. 🚶🌳

O Keep copy of final accounting. 🚶🌳

O Close estate bank account. 🚶🌳

Communications with Beneficiaries

O Provide final documentation to beneficiaries. 🚶

O Provide beneficiaries with document to release you from liability. 🚶

Chapter 4: Monthly & Weekly Organizer & Planner

The Weekly Planner

The weekly planner is your space to track what's happening with the estate and within you.

You can...

- Brain dump tasks for your week.

- Record reminders to check in with your basic needs.

- Check in with your trees (support people).

- Have a support person help you fill out the planner.

At the end of your day, you can...

- Look over what you accomplished and give yourself a hug, a high five, or a sticker.

- Check in with your body, mind, heart, and soul. What supported you today? What helped ease or hold your pain or decreased suffering?

- What do you need to give yourself permission to do, think, feel?

- Write yourself a permission slip as you end your day.

- Give yourself gold stars or stickers to support yourself and honor your hard work.

Example of end of the day check in:

What supported me today? What helped ease or hold my pain or decreased suffering?

I don't even know...taking my walk this morning was ok. At least I took it.

It just hurts so bad...but I did get a text message from my friend. They offered to help with laundry. I think that would help.

Space to reflect

What do you need to give yourself permission to do, think, feel?

I need to give myself permission to think this is awful and I hate it. I need permission to feel anger.

Mostly I need permission to accept my friend's offer to help with laundry.

Space to reflect

49

Bereavement and Estate Pilgrimage
First Month

**When grief rises and I feel lost or overwhelmed,
I will repeat:**

Who are my trees to support me?

Who are the forest rangers to guide me?

Basic Needs Tracker

Breathe Make your "out breath" longer than your "in breath" and keep breathing

Activity Move your body a little each day

Sleep and Rest

Identify your emotions and perhaps journal or talk into a phone to record, get emotions out.

Clean your body and bathe daily

Nature Spend time daily in fresh air and sun

Eat in regular intervals

Explore music, books, movies, TV shows

Drink water Try to drink 8-10 glasses a day

Stop and pull over while driving when a grief burst comes

Additional planner pages are available for free download at https://a-new-path.com/workbookresources/ or via the QR code at the back of the book.

Weekly Planner _____

	Monday	Tuesday	Wednesday
Tasks of Mourning/ Estate Work			
What professional help do I need?			
Tending to My Self: BASIC NEEDS			
Who of my friends and family can support me? What does that support look like?			
What felt supportive today/eased suffering?			
Permission Slip			

Month _____ **Year** _____

Thursday	Friday	Saturday/ Sunday

First Month Check-In

Congratulations! You survived the first month.

Even if it doesn't seem like you did a lot or you don't feel like celebrating, monthly check-ins with your grief and your journey are important places to pause. It's like you're stopping at a campground and taking stock. Congratulations and welcome to your first official check-in.

Journaling with Grief

What have you observed about your grief over the last month?

Reverse Bucket List

Make a list of what you've accomplished over the last month. Then take a moment to allow yourself to be with all the emotions that come. If your emotions are mixed, that makes sense…each item checked off the list represents your loss.

Taking with Me

What would you like to focus on or take with you over the next month? Is there an area that needs your attention? Are there people you want to ask for support? Has there been a practice or one of the BASIC NEEDS that has really resourced you?

Take a few moments and list what you most want to focus on for the next month. When overwhelmed, return to this page to remind yourself of your focus and your resource.

Bereavement and Estate Pilgrimage
Second Month

**When grief rises and I feel lost or overwhelmed,
I will repeat:**

Who are my trees to support me?

Who are the forest rangers to guide me?

Basic Needs Tracker

Breathe Make your "out breath" longer than your "in breath" and keep breathing

Activity Move your body a little each day

Sleep and Rest

Identify your emotions and perhaps journal or talk into a phone to record, get emotions out.

Clean your body and bathe daily

Nature Spend time daily in fresh air and sun

Eat in regular intervals

Explore music, books, movies, TV shows

Drink water Try to drink 8-10 glasses a day

Stop and pull over while driving when a grief burst comes

Estate To-Dos:

- ☒ Thank you notes for donations
- ○ Debts to settle
- ○ Probate information
- ○ Financial asset/life insurance information
- ○ Property/house needs
- ○ Death notifications to send

Space to reflect

Additional planner pages are available for free download at https://a-new-path.com/workbookresources/ or via the QR code at the back of the book.

Weekly Planner _____

	Monday	Tuesday	Wednesday
Tasks of Mourning/ Estate Work			
What professional help do I need?			
Tending to My Self: BASIC NEEDS			
Who of my friends and family can support me? What does that support look like?			
What felt supportive today/eased suffering?			
Permission Slip			

Month _____ **Year** _____

Thursday	Friday	Saturday/ Sunday

Second Month Check-In

Congratulations! You arrived at the end of your second month. It's time to stop at your next campsite for a moment.

Journaling with Grief

What have you observed about your grief over the last month?

Reverse Bucket List

Make a list of what you've accomplished over the last month. Then take a moment to allow yourself to be with all the emotions that come. If your emotions are mixed, that makes sense…each item checked off the list represents your loss.

Taking with Me

What would you like to focus on or take with you over the next month? Is there an area that needs your attention? Are there people you want to ask for support? Has there been a practice or one of the BASIC NEEDS that has really resourced you?

Take a few moments and list what you most want to focus on for the next month. When overwhelmed, return to this page to remind yourself of your focus and your resource.

Bereavement and Estate Pilgrimage
Third Month

When grief rises and I feel lost or overwhelmed, I will repeat:

Who are my trees to support me?

Who are the forest rangers to guide me?

Basic Needs Tracker

Breathe Make your "out breath" longer than your "in breath" and keep breathing

Activity Move your body a little each day

Sleep and Rest

Identify your emotions and perhaps journal or talk into a phone to record, get emotions out.

Clean your body and bathe daily

Nature Spend time daily in fresh air and sun

Eat in regular intervals

Explore music, books, movies, TV shows

Drink water Try to drink 8-10 glasses a day

Stop and pull over while driving when a grief burst comes

Estate To-Dos:

- ☒ Personal connections
- ○ Probate information
- ○ Finances (assets and debt information)
- ○ Property/house needs
- ○ Death notifications to send
- ○ Digital life/accounts

Space to reflect

Additional planner pages are available for free download at https://a-new-path.com/workbookresources/ or via the QR code at the back of the book.

Weekly Planner _____

	Monday	Tuesday	Wednesday
Tasks of Mourning/ Estate Work			
What professional help do I need?			
Tending to My Self: BASIC NEEDS			
Who of my friends and family can support me? What does that support look like?			
What felt supportive today/eased suffering?			
Permission Slip			

Month _____ **Year** _____

Thursday	Friday	Saturday/ Sunday

Third Month Check-In

Congratulations! You are ending your first quarter. Whether you're having all the feels or you're numb or a little bit of both, welcome!

Journaling with Grief

What have you observed about your grief over the last month?

Reverse Bucket List

Make a list of what you've accomplished over the last month. Then take a moment to allow yourself to be with all the emotions that come. If your emotions are mixed, that makes sense…each item checked off the list represents your loss.

Taking with Me

What would you like to focus on or take with you over the next month? Is there an area that needs your attention? Are there people you want to ask for support? Has there been a practice or one of the BASIC NEEDS that has really resourced you?

Take a few moments and list what you most want to focus on for the next month. When overwhelmed, return to this page to remind yourself of your focus and your resource.

Bereavement and Estate Pilgrimage
Fourth Month

When grief rises and I feel lost or overwhelmed, I will repeat:

Who are my trees to support me?

Who are the forest rangers to guide me?

Basic Needs Tracker

Breathe Make your "out breath" longer than your "in breath" and keep breathing

Activity Move your body a little each day

Sleep and Rest

Identify your emotions and perhaps journal or talk into a phone to record, get emotions out.

Clean your body and bathe daily

Nature Spend time daily in fresh air and sun

Eat in regular intervals

Explore music, books, movies, TV shows

Drink water Try to drink 8-10 glasses a day

Stop and pull over while driving when a grief burst comes

Estate To-Dos:

- ⊗ Personal connections
- ○ Probate information
- ○ Finances (assets and debt information)
- ○ Property/house needs
- ○ Death notifications to send
- ○ Digital life/accounts

Space to reflect

Additional planner pages are available for free download at https://a-new-path.com/workbookresources/ or via the QR code at the back of the book.

Weekly Planner _____

	Monday	Tuesday	Wednesday
Tasks of Mourning/ Estate Work			
What professional help do I need?			
Tending to My Self: BASIC NEEDS			
Who of my friends and family can support me? What does that support look like?			
What felt supportive today/eased suffering?			
Permission Slip			

Month _____ **Year** _____

Thursday	Friday	Saturday/ Sunday

Fourth Month Check-In

You've made it another month. You may not be feeling like congratulations at all. Still, I invite you to pause in this place. Take a moment to reflect on where you've been and where you want to go.

Journaling with Grief

What have you observed about your grief over the last month?

Reverse Bucket List

Make a list of what you've accomplished over the last month. Then take a moment to allow yourself to be with all the emotions that come. If your emotions are mixed, that makes sense...each item checked off the list represents your loss.

Taking with Me

What would you like to focus on or take with you over the next month? Is there an area that needs your attention? Are there people you want to ask for support? Has there been a practice or one of the BASIC NEEDS that has really resourced you?

Take a few moments and list what you most want to focus on for the next month. When overwhelmed, return to this page to remind yourself of your focus and your resource.

Bereavement and Estate Pilgrimage
Fifth Month

When grief rises and I feel lost or overwhelmed, I will repeat:

Who are my trees to support me?

Who are the forest rangers to guide me?

Basic Needs Tracker

Breathe Make your "out breath" longer than your "in breath" and keep breathing

Activity Move your body a little each day

Sleep and Rest

Identify your emotions and perhaps journal or talk into a phone to record, get emotions out.

Clean your body and bathe daily

Nature Spend time daily in fresh air and sun

Eat in regular intervals

Explore music, books, movies, TV shows

Drink Water Try to drink 8-10 glasses a day

Stop and pull over while driving when a grief burst comes

Estate To-Dos:

- ⊗ Personal connections
- ○ Probate information
- ○ Finances (assets and debt information)
- ○ Property/house needs
- ○ Death notifications to send
- ○ Digital life/accounts

Space to reflect

Additional planner pages are available for free download at https://a-new-path.com/workbookresources/ or via the QR code at the back of the book.

Weekly Planner _____

	Monday	Tuesday	Wednesday
Tasks of Mourning/ Estate Work			
What professional help do I need?			
Tending to My Self: BASIC NEEDS			
Who of my friends and family can support me? What does that support look like?			
What felt supportive today/eased suffering?			
Permission Slip			

Month _____ **Year**_____

Thursday	Friday	Saturday/ Sunday

Fifth Month Check-In

Welcome to your next moment to intentionally pause and reflect. Sometime real life and estate to-dos become so much that we haven't had time to really be with the grief of our loss. Or we can be so deep in it that it can feel like grief will always be the center of our world. Perhaps it's a little bit of both. Take a moment to check in with yourself and your process.

Journaling with Grief

What have you observed about your grief over the last month?

Reverse Bucket List

Make a list of what you've accomplished over the last month. Then take a moment to allow yourself to be with all the emotions that come. If your emotions are mixed, that makes sense…each item checked off the list represents your loss.

Taking with Me

What would you like to focus on or take with you over the next month? Is there an area that needs your attention? Are there people you want to ask for support? Has there been a practice or one of the BASIC NEEDS that has really resourced you?

Take a few moments and list what you most want to focus on for the next month. When overwhelmed, return to this page to remind yourself of your focus and your resource.

Bereavement and Estate Pilgrimage
Sixth Month

**When grief rises and I feel lost or overwhelmed,
I will repeat:**

Who are my trees to support me?

Who are the forest rangers to guide me?

Basic Needs Tracker

Breathe Make your "out breath" longer than your "in breath" and keep breathing

Activity Move your body a little each day

Sleep and Rest

Identify your emotions and perhaps journal or talk into a phone to record, get emotions out.

Clean your body and bathe daily

Nature Spend time daily in fresh air and sun

Eat in regular intervals

Explore music, books, movies, TV shows

Drink water Try to drink 8-10 glasses a day

Stop and pull over while driving when a grief burst comes

Estate To-Dos:

- ⊘ Personal connections
- ○ Probate information
- ○ Finances (assets and debt information)
- ○ Property/house needs
- ○ Death notifications to send
- ○ Digital life/accounts

Space to reflect

Additional planner pages are available for free download at https://a-new-path.com/workbookresources/ or via the QR code at the back of the book.

Weekly Planner _____

	Monday	*Tuesday*	*Wednesday*
Tasks of Mourning/ Estate Work			
What professional help do I need?			
Tending to My Self: BASIC NEEDS			
Who of my friends and family can support me? What does that support look like?			
What felt supportive today/eased suffering?			
Permission Slip			

Month _____ **Year**_____

Thursday	Friday	Saturday/ Sunday

Sixth Month Check-In

Congratulations! You are ending your second quarter/
half of the year. Is that hard to believe? Do you feel like
it's been an eternity or like no time has passed? Or
perhaps, a little bit of both.

Journaling with Grief

What have you observed about your grief over
the last month?

Reverse Bucket List

Make a list of what you've accomplished over the last month.
Then take a moment to allow yourself to be with all the
emotions that come. If your emotions are mixed, that makes
sense…each item checked off the list represents your loss.

Taking with Me

What would you like to focus on or take with you over the next month? Is there an area that needs your attention? Are there people you want to ask for support? Has there been a practice or one of the BASIC NEEDS that has really resourced you?

Take a few moments and list what you most want to focus on for the next month. When overwhelmed, return to this page to remind yourself of your focus and your resource.

Bereavement and Estate Pilgrimage
Seventh Month

When grief rises and I feel lost or overwhelmed, I will repeat:

Who are my trees to support me?

Who are the forest rangers to guide me?

Basic Needs Tracker

Breathe Make your "out breath" longer than your "in breath" and keep breathing

Activity Move your body a little each day

Sleep and Rest

Identify your emotions and perhaps journal or talk into a phone to record, get emotions out.

Clean your body and bathe daily

Nature Spend time daily in fresh air and sun

Eat in regular intervals

Explore music, books, movies, TV shows

Drink water Try to drink 8-10 glasses a day

Stop and pull over while driving when a grief burst comes

Estate To-Dos:

- ☒ Personal connections
- ○ Probate information
- ○ Finances (assets and debt information)
- ○ Property/house needs
- ○ Death notifications to send
- ○ Digital life/accounts

Space to reflect

Additional planner pages are available for free download at https://a-new-path.com/workbookresources/ or via the QR code at the back of the book.

Weekly Planner _____

	Monday	Tuesday	Wednesday
Tasks of Mourning/ Estate Work			
What professional help do I need?			
Tending to My Self: BASIC NEEDS			
Who of my friends and family can support me? What does that support look like?			
What felt supportive today/eased suffering?			
Permission Slip			

Month _____ **Year** _____

Thursday	Friday	Saturday/ Sunday

Seventh Month Check-In

Welcome to your seventh month pause.

Journaling with Grief

What have you observed about your grief over
the last month?

Reverse Bucket List

Make a list of what you've accomplished over the last month.
Then take a moment to allow yourself to be with all the
emotions that come. If your emotions are mixed, that makes
sense...each item checked off the list represents your loss.

Taking with Me

What would you like to focus on or take with you over the next month? Is there an area that needs your attention? Are there people you want to ask for support? Has there been a practice or one of the BASIC NEEDS that has really resourced you?

Take a few moments and list what you most want to focus on for the next month. When overwhelmed, return to this page to remind yourself of your focus and your resource.

Bereavement and Estate Pilgrimage
Eighth Month

**When grief rises and I feel lost or overwhelmed,
I will repeat:**

Who are my trees to support me?

Who are the forest rangers to guide me?

Basic Needs Tracker

Breathe Make your "out breath" longer than your "in breath" and keep breathing

Activity Move your body a little each day

Sleep and Rest

Identify your emotions and perhaps journal or talk into a phone to record, get emotions out.

Clean your body and bathe daily

Nature Spend time daily in fresh air and sun

Eat in regular intervals

Explore music, books, movies, TV shows

Drink water Try to drink 8-10 glasses a day

Stop and pull over while driving when a grief burst comes

Estate To-Dos:

- ☒ Personal connections
- ○ Probate information
- ○ Finances (assets and debt information)
- ○ Property/house needs
- ○ Digital life/accounts

Space to reflect

Additional planner pages are available for free download
at https://a-new-path.com/workbookresources/ or via the
QR code at the back of the book.

Weekly Planner _____

	Monday	*Tuesday*	*Wednesday*
Tasks of Mourning/ Estate Work			
What professional help do I need?			
Tending to My Self: BASIC NEEDS			
Who of my friends and family can support me? What does that support look like?			
What felt supportive today/eased suffering?			
Permission Slip			

Month _____ **Year** _____

Thursday	Friday	Saturday/ Sunday

Eighth Month Check-In

Welcome to your eighth month pause.

Journaling with Grief

What have you observed about your grief over
the last month?

Reverse Bucket List

Make a list of what you've accomplished over the last month.
Then take a moment to allow yourself to be with all the
emotions that come. If your emotions are mixed, that makes
sense...each item checked off the list represents your loss.

Taking with Me

What would you like to focus on or take with you over the next month? Is there an area that needs your attention? Are there people you want to ask for support? Has there been a practice or one of the BASIC NEEDS that has really resourced you?

Take a few moments and list what you most want to focus on for the next month. When overwhelmed, return to this page to remind yourself of your focus and your resource.

Bereavement and Estate Pilgrimage
Ninth Month

When grief rises and I feel lost or overwhelmed, I will repeat:

Who are my trees to support me?

Who are the forest rangers to guide me?

Basic Needs Tracker

Breathe Make your "out breath" longer than your "in breath" and keep breathing

Activity Move your body a little each day

Sleep and Rest

Identify your emotions and perhaps journal or talk into a phone to record, get emotions out.

Clean your body and bathe daily

Nature Spend time daily in fresh air and sun

Eat in regular intervals

Explore music, books, movies, TV shows

Drink water Try to drink 8-10 glasses a day

Stop and pull over while driving when a grief burst comes

Estate To-Dos:

- ☒ Personal connections
- ○ Probate information
- ○ Finances (assets and debt information)
- ○ Property/house needs
- ○ Digital life/accounts

Space to reflect

Additional planner pages are available for free download at https://a-new-path.com/workbookresources/ or via the QR code at the back of the book.

Weekly Planner _____

	Monday	Tuesday	Wednesday
Tasks of Mourning/ Estate Work			
What professional help do I need?			
Tending to My Self: BASIC NEEDS			
Who of my friends and family can support me? What does that support look like?			
What felt supportive today/eased suffering?			
Permission Slip			

Month _____ **Year**_____

Thursday	Friday	Saturday/ Sunday

Ninth Month Check-In

You have survived nine months. That's right. It's the end of the third quarter. Perhaps the month ahead has some big logistical ending. Or perhaps your logistical process is longer and you're struggling to see the light at the end of the tunnel. Or a little bit of both.

Journaling with Grief

What have you observed about your grief over the last month?

Reverse Bucket List

Make a list of what you've accomplished over the last month. Then take a moment to allow yourself to be with all the emotions that come. If your emotions are mixed, that makes sense...each item checked off the list represents your loss.

Taking with Me

What would you like to focus on or take with you over the next month? Is there an area that needs your attention? Are there people you want to ask for support? Has there been a practice or one of the BASIC NEEDS that has really resourced you?

Take a few moments and list what you most want to focus on for the next month. When overwhelmed, return to this page to remind yourself of your focus and your resource.

Bereavement and Estate Pilgrimage
Tenth Month

When grief rises and I feel lost or overwhelmed, I will repeat:

Who are my trees to support me?

Who are the forest rangers to guide me?

Basic Needs Tracker

Breathe Make your "out breath" longer than your "in breath" and keep breathing

Activity Move your body a little each day

Sleep and Rest

Identify your emotions and perhaps journal or talk into a phone to record, get emotions out.

Clean your body and bathe daily

Nature Spend time daily in fresh air and sun

Eat in regular intervals

Explore music, books, movies, TV shows

Drink water Try to drink 8-10 glasses a day

Stop and pull over while driving when a grief burst comes

Estate To-Dos:

- ☒ Personal connections
- ○ Probate information
- ○ Finances (assets and debt information)
- ○ Property/house needs
- ○ Digital life/accounts

Space to reflect

Additional planner pages are available for free download at https://a-new-path.com/workbookresources/ or via the QR code at the back of the book.

Weekly Planner _____

	Monday	*Tuesday*	*Wednesday*
Tasks of Mourning/ Estate Work			
What professional help do I need?			
Tending to My Self: BASIC NEEDS			
Who of my friends and family can support me? What does that support look like?			
What felt supportive today/eased suffering?			
Permission Slip			

Month _____ **Year**_____

Thursday	Friday	Saturday/ Sunday

Tenth Month Check-In

Welcome to your tenth month check-in.

Journaling with Grief

What have you observed about your grief over
the last month?

Reverse Bucket List

Make a list of what you've accomplished over the last month.
Then take a moment to allow yourself to be with all the
emotions that come. If your emotions are mixed, that makes
sense…each item checked off the list represents your loss.

Taking with Me

What would you like to focus on or take with you over the next month? Is there an area that needs your attention? Are there people you want to ask for support? Has there been a practice or one of the BASIC NEEDS that has really resourced you?

Take a few moments and list what you most want to focus on for the next month. When overwhelmed, return to this page to remind yourself of your focus and your resource.

Bereavement and Estate Pilgrimage
Eleventh Month

When grief rises and I feel lost or overwhelmed, I will repeat:

Who are my trees to support me?

Who are the forest rangers to guide me?

Basic Needs Tracker

Breathe Make your "out breath" longer than your "in breath" and keep breathing

Activity Move your body a little each day

Sleep and Rest

Identify your emotions and perhaps journal or talk into a phone to record, get emotions out.

Clean your body and bathe daily

Nature Spend time daily in fresh air and sun

Eat in regular intervals

Explore music, books, movies, TV shows

Drink water Try to drink 8-10 glasses a day

Stop and pull over while driving when a grief burst comes

Estate To-Dos:

- ☒ Personal connections
- ○ Probate information
- ○ Finances (assets and debt information)
- ○ Property/house needs
- ○ Digital life/accounts

Space to reflect

Additional planner pages are available for free download at https://a-new-path.com/workbookresources/ or via the QR code at the back of the book.

Weekly Planner _____

	Monday	*Tuesday*	*Wednesday*
Tasks of Mourning/ Estate Work			
What professional help do I need?			
Tending to My Self: BASIC NEEDS			
Who of my friends and family can support me? What does that support look like?			
What felt supportive today/eased suffering?			
Permission Slip			

Month _____ **Year** _____

Thursday	Friday	Saturday/ Sunday

Eleventh Month Check-In

Welcome to your eleventh check-in.

Journaling with Grief

What have you observed about your grief over the last month?

Reverse Bucket List

Make a list of what you've accomplished over the last month. Then take a moment to allow yourself to be with all the emotions that come. If your emotions are mixed, that makes sense...each item checked off the list represents your loss.

Taking with Me

What would you like to focus on or take with you over the next month? Is there an area that needs your attention? Are there people you want to ask for support? Has there been a practice or one of the BASIC NEEDS that has really resourced you?

Take a few moments and list what you most want to focus on for the next month. When overwhelmed, return to this page to remind yourself of your focus and your resource.

Bereavement and Estate Pilgrimage
Twelfth Month

When grief rises and I feel lost or overwhelmed, I will repeat:

Who are my trees to support me?

Who are the forest rangers to guide me?

Basic Needs Tracker

Breathe Make your "out breath" longer than your "in breath" and keep breathing

Activity Move your body a little each day

Sleep and Rest

Identify your emotions and perhaps journal or talk into a phone to record, get emotions out.

Clean your body and bathe daily

Nature Spend time daily in fresh air and sun

Eat in regular intervals

Explore music, books, movies, TV shows

Drink water Try to drink 8-10 glasses a day

Stop and pull over while driving when a grief burst comes

Estate To-Dos:

- ☒ Personal connections
- ○ Probate information
- ○ Finances (assets and debt information)
- ○ Property/house needs
- ○ Digital life/accounts

Space to reflect

Additional planner pages are available for free download at https://a-new-path.com/workbookresources/ or via the QR code at the back of the book.

Weekly Planner _____

	Monday	*Tuesday*	*Wednesday*
Tasks of Mourning/ Estate Work			
What professional help do I need?			
Tending to My Self: BASIC NEEDS			
Who of my friends and family can support me? What does that support look like?			
What felt supportive today/ eased suffering?			
Permission Slip			

Month _____ **Year** _____

Thursday	Friday	Saturday/ Sunday

Twelfth Month Check-In

Welcome to your twelfth month check-in. You survived one full year. Yes, you did. Maybe you didn't think you could do it. Or maybe you have found yourself counting down the days to today and thought the grief would be gone—but it's not. Maybe your logistical work is already finished and you're living a life without your person and their estate. Maybe you're recognizing that your person is gone. Now that the firsts are over, you have the seconds. But the logistical realities linger—you're weary and ready for them to be done. Wherever you are and however you are, take a moment to check in. Perhaps look back at how far you've traveled.

Journaling with Grief

What have you observed about your grief over the last month?

Reverse Bucket List

Make a list of what you've accomplished over the last month. Then take a moment to allow yourself to be with all the emotions that come. If your emotions are mixed, that makes sense...each item checked off the list represents your loss.

Taking with Me

What would you like to focus on or take with you over the next month? Is there an area that needs your attention? Are there people you want to ask for support? Has there been a practice or one of the BASIC NEEDS that has really resourced you?

Take a few moments and list what you most want to focus on for the next month. When overwhelmed, return to this page to remind yourself of your focus and your resource.

Chapter 5: More Practices & Education About Grief

In addition to the stressors of bereavement and adjusting to your new role, you will also need to navigate different systems where you have little control over "checking something off the to-do list."

Many times, closing an account or distributing an asset has multiple steps, and you won't know all of them until you have actually accomplished the task.

To help with the frustration of this, you can shift your goal from accomplishing the task (out of your control) to something else like working on a project for 30 minutes (in your control).

Emily and Amelia Nagoski, the authors of Burnout: *The Secret to Unlocking the Stress Cycle,* call this **Re-Defining Winning.**

Here are a few possible goals when your to-do list involves tasks with unknown timelines or steps:

- Work for x amount of minutes/hours.

- Engage stress discharge practices 5 times in the process of working on estate.

- Have one of your trees (support people) with you.

- Text one of your trees (support people) before and after your estate work to check in.

- Count the number of times the phone rings until you get a person on the line.

Guess how many minutes you will be on hold.

Imagine the process as a game. Create a character to be and think of this as a quest.

Here are a few possible goals for when you get a person on the phone:

- Write down the name of the person and contact information if they can share that.

- Learn what the next step in the process is.

- Ask what advice they would give you.

- Ask and write down suggestions for how to access a person directly.

- Ask and write down the process for having your attorney, paralegal, accountant, or after loss professional call in your place.

When you're on hold and in the automated system maze, pick a few of the stress cycle disruptor practices. Highlight the ones your body/mind/spirit prefers.

Stress Cycle Disruptors

1. Sipping Breath

- Purse your lips like you would drink through a straw.
- "Drink" in 4 short breaths.
- Close your mouth.
- Breathe out slowly through your nose.

Repeat breath pattern 5-10 times. If counting is difficult, focus on short "in breath" through the mouth and longer "out breath" through the nose.

2. Full Body Tense and Relax

- Take a deep breath in with your mouth so that you fill your lungs.
- Hold your breath.
- While holding your breath, tense your muscles from head to toe: face, arms, hands, legs, feet.
- Hold breath and body for 5-10 seconds.
- Relax your body and slowly exhale.

This practice helps you quickly shift from fight/flight (sympathetic activation) back to a more relaxed state (parasympathetic). If you feel anxious before an event or encounter, doing this quickly can help you discharge extra energy and become more present.

3. Shake It Out

- Breathe as you normally do.
- Stand up.
- Shake your body by moving your arms, head, and torso.

If you are leaving a situation where you can tell you've been activated, your mind says, "I'm ok," but your body says, "I've got a lot of energy. I am not ok." Our stress response always gives us excess energy, and this is a quick and safe way to discharge it.

4. Hand on Stomach and Heart

- Place one hand on your stomach.

- Place the other hand on your heart.

- Experiment with left and right hands–different people have different preferences.

- Take 2-3 intentional breaths.

This practice is helpful when you find yourself getting pulled into the anxious energy of a situation or someone else's distress. It is a way of letting your body know that you are with you. It also helps you stay present and grounded in and with your own body.

5. Havening

There are three ways to haven.

- Gently rub the palms of your hands together. You want to feel a little pressure.

- Cross your arms over your chest. Gently rub your arm from your shoulder to your elbow. Again, you want to feel a little pressure.

- Gently rub your fingertips on your face–your cheeks, chin, and forehead. Again, you want to feel a little pressure.

This calming strategy is a great way to soothe your body and feel some support. Perhaps you are not completely triggered, but your body is tense. Havening can support you throughout the day.

6. Hugging to Relax

- For self-regulation

  - Cross arms over chest.

  - Hold on to outer arms.

  - Give yourself a big hug.

  - Breathe deeply. Really notice the sensations of holding and being with yourself.

- For co-regulation

  - Give spouse or child a hug.

  - Breathe deeply. (You may notice your body feeling a little anxious. Allow that to happen and simply breathe.)

  - Notice how it is as your body relaxes into the hug of the other person.

Hugging to relax for self-regulation helps us love and care for ourselves. It is also a good calming strategy to help us affirm our own physical boundaries. With spouses and children, hugging to relax helps us co-regulate one another. Just as anxiety is contagious, so is relaxation. This calming strategy can help soothe the nervous system faster than words.

** Some folks like to engage these practices and visualize themselves in a quest/journey like *Wonder Woman, Black Panther, Lord of the Rings,* or in games like *Super Mario Brothers.* The combination of physiological discharge and visualization can help you come back to yourself, your agency, and your empowerment.

What is a Dual Role and Are You in One?

A dual role is when you play different roles with the same person. Imagine that you wear different hats for different roles. You may have multiple hats; changing them takes extra brain capacity.

Here are a few of the "hats" you may be wearing:

- Child of your person (one role)

- Beneficiary of your person's stuff (another role)

- Sibling to other beneficiaries (yet another role)

- Executor/administrator (another role)

Here's a brief summary of the roles of Executor and Beneficiary:

Executor:

- An executor is a person appointed in a will to carry out the deceased person's wishes and manage the distribution of their assets.

- The executor is responsible for handling various tasks, including gathering and managing the deceased person's assets, paying debts and taxes, and distributing the remaining assets to the beneficiaries according to the terms of the will.

Beneficiary:

- A beneficiary is an individual or entity designated to receive assets or benefits from the deceased person's estate.

- Beneficiaries are entitled to inherit specific assets or a share of the estate, as outlined in the deceased person's will.

Having the responsibility of executor can sometimes conflict with your wants and needs as a beneficiary. Sometimes the wishes of your deceased person conflict with beneficiaries. As the executor, you may find yourself feeling caught in the middle...because you ARE!

Spaces Where Most Executors Feel the Pinch of the Dual Role

Conflict of Interest: The executor's duty to act in the best interests of all beneficiaries may conflict with their personal interest in maximizing their own share of the estate.

Impartiality Concerns: Other beneficiaries may question the impartiality of an executor who is also a beneficiary, raising concerns about fair and just distribution.

Legal and Ethical Considerations: Some jurisdictions may have rules or guidelines to address the potential conflicts that arise when an executor is also a beneficiary.

One of the largest contributors to chronic stress is role confusion and/or dual roles. No, you aren't losing your mind. Stress is a normal response to the place you find yourself.

Stress, Bereavement, and Estate Settlement

Stressor: an event, situation, person, memory, or thought that activates the stress response cycle

Stress: physiological reaction when your body/mind perceives threat or danger

Chronic stressor: ongoing/every day stressors that can't easily get "checked off the list"

Bereavement and estate settlement are chronic stressors.

How do I live with chronic stressors?

When we live in a situation filled with chronic stressors, we need quick discharge practices, soothing and discharging supports, and nourishment. Here are a few to try.

Quick Ways to Discharge and Soothe	Planned Practices to Discharge and/or Soothe	Nourish (What Fills Your Cup)
Tense and release	Meditation/prayer	
Make exhale longer than inhale	Movement (walk, yoga, box, dance, bike, swim, Zumba, pickleball)	Maybe anything from the previous lists... notice what happens in you when you engage practice
Focus on peripheral vision	Physical affection	
Shake it out	Gardening, forest bathing, spending time in nature	
Havening, self-hug, hug with trusted people	Creating, singing, art-ing	
Ground and orient	Connection with people	
Splash cold water on face, ice cube on wrist	Journaling and free writing	

Secondary Losses

As you move through the pilgrimage of the first year of bereavement, you might notice that the landscape is changing. Not only is your person not traveling with you, but you might also discover that the landmarks that used to be part of your life are now gone.

These additional losses are known as secondary losses. And we grieve those too.

Here are a few possible secondary losses.
Circle or highlight ones that you have experienced.

House/Home/ Moving	Connection and intimacy	Friendship
Financial security/ stability	Self-confidence	Roles with family and friends
Belief system and faith	Changes in work	Loss of the planned future
Loss of hopes and dreams	Sense of security/ safety of world	

Prepare to Journal

- Set a timer for 10-20 minutes.

- Light a candle.

- Place one hand on your heart and one on your stomach as you breathe slowly while gazing at the candles.

- If it is right for you, you can invoke Source/God/Love/ Higher Power/Universe to be with you today and through this time. You may also offer gratitude to your loved ones and to Source for their presence and support.

Here are some possible prompts…

I thought my life would be/look like….

I also miss…

I look in the mirror and I wonder…

The world can seem…

When I try to pray or go to my faith community…

Closing

Take a few moments to notice your breath. Don't try to make it be any different. Simply notice it.

If it's right for you and your body, notice the sensation of your feet touching the floor. Allow yourself to feel how gravity supports your body.

Chapter 6: Resources for Settling Your Person's Affairs

Glossary of Terms

When I became the administrator for my parents' estates, one of the many challenging aspects was the language barrier between the professionals who were helping me and my own knowledge. I felt like I was a kindergartner on the first day of school looking for my cubby where I could put my book bag. The conversation and decisions I needed to have were like reading Chaucer or Shakespeare, in terms of difficulty.

Below are some basic definitions and explanations. As always, this is a general overview so please do consult with your professional team—your forest rangers—for specific information for your unique situation.

Administrator: a person appointed by the court to manage the estate and make sure all the debts are paid and assets are distributed to the beneficiaries. (This is if the deceased had no will or their will is not seen as valid.)

Asset: everything that belongs to a person at the time they die: physical belongings like real estate, cars, furniture, bank account, retirement account, investments, digital belongings/ creations, and intellectual property.

Beneficiary: the person, charity, or entity that receives specific assets or benefits from their person's estate. Beneficiaries are listed in wills, trusts, life insurance policies, and some investment accounts like IRAs.

Beneficiary or Inherited IRA: an IRA that you inherit from a person who has died. It can be moved into a new IRA for the inheritor or beneficiary. In 2020, the US passed a law called the SECURE Act that changed some of the rules.

Estate: everything that a deceased person owned.

Estate Bank Account: special bank account for the deceased's liquid assets. This is the bank account that pays out any debts, and liquid assets are distributed from it.

Estate Inventory: detailed list of all of the assets and all of the liabilities (debts) that make up a deceased person's estate.

Executor: person appointed in the will to manage the estate, make sure all the debts are paid, and assets are distributed to the beneficiaries.

Executor's Fee: compensation paid to the executor for their work in managing and settling the estate. Often the payment is a percentage of the estate's total value or a flat fee.

Fiduciary: a trusted person or company with the legal authority to manage another's property, and the duty to act in that person's best interest (includes executors/administrators and personal representatives).

Guardian: an individual appointed to care for and make decisions on behalf of minor children or incapacitated adults in the event of the parent's or guardian's death.

Heir: someone who is set to inherit the property of the deceased when no will or testament has been made; usually they are a close family member.

Intestate: when your person dies without a will or without a will that is valid in court, then their assets get distributed by the law in the place the deceased lived.

Liability: debts or money that your person owed such as medical bills, credit card debt, or mortgage on a house.

Life Insurance: a contract that your person (the policy owner) had with a life insurance company; beneficiaries receive the money upon the policy owner's death.

Medallion Signature: fancy confirmation of someone's signature, performed at many banks for a small fee.

Probate: the legal process for validating someone's will, settling their current financial affairs like paying off debts and paying final taxes, and distributing assets to beneficiaries.

Required Minimum Distribution (RMD): the minimum amount of money that must be withdrawn from an IRA/SEP IRA. In the US, there have been many changes with the law starting with the SECURE Act in 2020, so if you have to deal with this, estate accountants and financial advisors can help.

Short Certificate: a legal document that gives the executor, administrator, or personal representative the legal authority to deal with assets.

Taxes: the terms inheritance tax and estate tax are sometimes used interchangeably. In the US, different states have different rules about inheritance tax.

Testator: a person who dies with a will.

Trust: a legal entity that holds people's assets. There are many different kinds, and this is where financial and estate professionals help you out. Most times people choose trusts to avoid probate and to help assets pass along more smoothly.

**Adapted from Glossary of Estate Planning Terms by the American Bar Association
https://www.americanbar.org/groups/real_property_trust_estate/re-sources/estate-planning/glossary/

Is There a Difference Between the Estate and Probate?

YES! It's kind of like rectangles and squares. All squares are rectangles, but not all rectangles are squares. Or all trauma has grief, but not all grief is traumatic. All people who die will have an estate. But not everyone who dies will have assets (belongings) that need to go through probate.

An estate is a thing, whereas probate is a process. Here's a quick summary: Estate and probate are terms often used in the context of someone's financial and legal affairs after they pass away. While they are related, they have distinct meanings:

Estate: An estate is everything a person possesses or owns, including their debt, their ideas (intellectual property), and their data (think digital life AKA social media). Their prized possessions, Pokémon card collection, journals, and family heirlooms are all part of the estate. They go along with what people commonly think of in an estate–their money and house. You will hear the terms assets (their belongings, real estate, bank accounts, investments, personal effects) and liabilities (their debts).

When someone passes away, they can no longer manage or make decisions about their stuff. So that's why their stuff becomes a separate legal entity called an estate. The estate gets an EIN number and is like a business that gets managed by a person. (More on this later.)

Probate: Probate is a legal process that takes place after someone's death to make sure their property is given away correctly and their debts are paid off. If there is a will, probate is also the process that makes sure the will is valid. The court oversees the probate process which involves many steps that are different depending upon where your person lived. This is why having an estate attorney familiar with the probate process in your person's home state can be super helpful. The primary goal of probate is to provide a structured and legal way to transfer ownership of assets and settle financial matters after someone's death.

TL/DR:

- Estates are the title given to people's stuff after they die.

- Probate is the legal process for dividing up the stuff.

Tools Available to Help You Stay Organized

You don't have to create your own organizational system. Here are several options.

Name	Method	Details
NOK (Next of Kin) BOX (Nokbox.com)	Physical organizer to store, track, and organize all aspects of your person's affairs	Each labeled file folder includes: • Instructions • Graphic organizers to document information • Checklist for documenting progress • Space for notes
Executor.org	Online secure data vault to track and store data about physical, financial, and non-financial assets	Includes: • Series of videos explaining steps of probate process • Brief overview of probate process • Data vault to keep track of physical, financial, and non-financial assets
Everplans	Online HIPPA compliant digital vault to secure, organize, and share important information	App that allows you to upload and store documents. Paid subscription allows for more data and sharing.
Trustworthy (Trustworthy.com)	Digital vault to secure, organize, and share important information	Includes: • Encrypted app where documents can be stored and uploaded • Sharing feature to allow sharing to different people • Email feature
Sought	App to help categorize and gift personal items of both financial value and sentimental value	Includes: • Ability to inventory belongings • Track belongings with photos • Print and customize reports

Sample Death Notification Letter to Utility Companies and State/Local Agencies

It is recommended that you send a letter with a copy of the death certificate and a copy of your authority to administrate the estate, because email is not a secure way to send information.

> Your Name
> Your Street Address
> Your City, State, Zip Code
> Your Email Address
> Your Phone Number
>
> The Date
>
> Recipient Name (if you have one)
> Utility Companies/State/Local Agencies
> Their Street Address
> Their City, State, Zip Code

Subject: Death Notification of (Your Person's Full Name)

Dear _____ ,

I am writing to inform you of the passing of (Your Person's Full Name), who was an account holder/customer/resident with your institution. They passed away on (Date of Death).

Below are the details pertaining to the deceased individual:
> Full Name:
> Date of Birth:
> Date of Death:

Please find the enclosed copy of their death certificate for your records, as well as a copy of (legal document that authorizes you to act on behalf of your person's estate).

Sample Death Notification Letter to Utility Companies and State/Local Agencies (cont.)

I kindly request your assistance in updating your records and handling the necessary administrative tasks related to (Your Person's) accounts with (Name of Institution/ Agency). Please provide me the specific forms or procedures for transferring the responsibility of the account to (the Estate of Your Person) at your earliest convenience. OR Please send me a confirmation that this account has been closed at your earliest convenience.

Sincerely,
Your Full Name

Sample Death Notification Letter to Financial Institutions

Your Name
Your Street Address
Your City, State, Zip Code
Your Email Address
Your Phone Number

The Date

Recipient Name (if you have one) or Transition Office/Estate Services
Financial Institution
Their Street Address
Their City, State, Zip Code

Subject: Death Notification of (Your Person's Full Name)

Dear _____ ,

I am writing to inform you of the passing of (Your Person's Full Name), who was an account holder/with your institution. They passed away on (Date of Death).

Below are the details pertaining to the deceased individual:

    Full Name:

    Date of Birth:

    Date of Death:

Please find the enclosed copy of their death certificate for your records, as well as a copy of (legal document that authorizes you to act on behalf of your person's estate).

I kindly request your assistance in updating your records and handling the necessary administrative tasks related to (Your Person's) accounts with your institution. If there are specific forms or procedures that need to be followed, please provide them at your earliest convenience.

If there are any outstanding balances, please let me know the procedures for settling them or transferring the assets, if applicable.

Please reach out to me at (Your Phone Number) or (Your Email Address) if there is any additional information/documentation required.

Thank you for your understanding and cooperation during this difficult time.

Sincerely,

Your Full Name

Sample Chart for Tracking All Debt/Payment Accounts (These are for any that had financial information or purchases.)

Account	Due Date	Amount Due	Date Sent Death Notification	Date Account Closed

Sample Chart for Tracking All Financial Assets

Financial Institution	Account Type/#	Amount	Beneficiary	Probate Y/N	Date Transferred to Estate or Beneficiary

Sample Form for Tracking Bank Accounts

Financial Institution:
Contact Name
Contact Phone Number
Contact Email

Best Way to Contact People with this Institution:

Type of Account:

Checking   Savings   Money Market/CDs

The account is: *(circle one)*

Jointly Owned   Payable on Death

Living Trust   Soley Owned

Account Number:

Find and Locate:
- Debit Card
- Checks
- Deposit Slips
- Withdrawal Slips
- Statements

Notes About This Account and Financial Institution:

Sample Script for Talking with Financial Institutions

If you don't know some of this information, you will need to call the financial institution and ask to speak with either the branch manager or the transition department.

> *Good morning/afternoon, my name is*
> *_____, and I am the executor/*
> *administrator for _____ 's estate.*
> *I'm calling in reference to their account with you.*
>
> *May I have your name and your number?*

Often the reply will ask you to verify your identity and your person's identity, so have the death certificate and a copy of the account readily accessible to reference.

> *Would you please inform me whether this account*
> *is Jointly Owned, Payable on Death, Living Trust,*
> *or Solely Owned?*
>
> *Thank you. What are the next steps in closing this*
> *account and/or transferring the funds?*

-
-
-

Summarize the steps back to the person to verify what you heard.

> *Thank you. If I have a problem with the steps above,*
> *whom do I contact and how do I best contact them?*

167

Sample Form for Tracking Investment Accounts

Financial Institution or Brokerage Firm:
Contact Name
Contact Phone Number
Contact Email

Best Way to Contact People with this Institution:

Type of Account: and Account Numbers:

O Retirement (IRA, Roth IRA, SEP IRA)

O Employer Plans (401K; 403B; Pension)

O Investment Account

O Annuities

O Cryptocurrency

O College Savings

O Individual Stocks

O Individual Bonds

Beneficiary Names and Contact Information:

Notes About This Account and Financial Institution:

Sample Form for Beneficiary Contact Information

Name	Address	Email & Phone	Relationship/ Other Information

References and Resources

Henley, Patricia. *The Hummingbird House.* MacMurray, 1999.

Grief Resources

Devine, Megan. It*'s Okay That You're Not Okay: Meeting Grief and Loss in a Culture that Doesn't Understand.* Sounds True Adult, 2017.

Johnson, Michelle Cassandra. *Finding Refuge: Heart Work for Healing Collective Grief.* Shambhala, 2021.

Kessler, David. *Finding Meaning: The Sixth Stage of Grief* Scribner, 2019.

O'Connor, Mary-Frances. *The Grieving Brain: The Surprising Science of How We Learn from Love and Loss.* HarperOne, 2022.

Stroebe, Margaret, and Henk Schut. *The Dual Process Model of Coping with Bereavement: Rationale and Description in Death Studies,* vol. 23, no. 3, 1999, pp. 197-224, https://pubmed.ncbi.nlm.nih.gov/10848151/.

Weller, Frances. *The Wild Edge of Sorrow: Rituals of Renewal and the Sacred Work of Grief.* North Atlantic Books, 2015.

Wolfelt, Alan D. *Understanding Your Grief: Ten Essential Touchstones for Finding Hope and Healing Your Heart.* Companion Press, 2021.

Worden, William. *The Tasks of Mourning in Grief Counseling and Grief TherapyFinding Refuge,* 5th ed. Springer, 2018.

After Loss Logistics

Everplans Team. Settling an Estate.
https://www.everplans.com/settling-an-estate.

Glossary of Estate Planning Terms by the American
Bar Association https://www.americanbar.org/groups/real_
property_trust_estate/resources/estate-planning/glossary/

Hannibal, Betsy Simmons. *How to Settle an Estate: If
You're the Executor of an Estate, Here's What You Need
to Do.* https://www.nolo.com/legal-encyclopedia/how-set-
tle-estate.html.

Murphy, Katheryn, and Margaret Munro.
Estate and Trust Administration for Dummies

O'Brien, Patrick. *Fifteen Primary Duties of an Executor.*
https://executor.org/resource/duties-of-an-executor/.

Randolph, Mary. T*he Executor's Guide: Settling a Loved
One's Estate or Trust (6th Edition).* NOLO, 2014.

Professionals After Loss. *What to Do After Loss and How
an After Loss Professional Can Help.*

Stewart, Cianna. *Dying Kindness Podcast.*

Stress and Trauma

Fay, Deirdre. *Becoming Safely Embodied: A Guide to
Organize Your Mind, Body and Heart to Feel Secure
in the World.* Morgan James Publishing, 2021.

Nagoski, Emily, and Amelia Nagoski. *Burnout: The Secret
to Unlocking the Stress Cycle.* Ballantine Books, 2019.

Disclaimer

Take good care

Wherever you are in your grief and after-loss journey, may you know that you are not alone. Please know that although grief and logistics are often solitary work, none of us can walk the path alone. If you seek more support, please reach out.

With you on your journey.

M. M.

Megan Malick
www.a-new-path.com

Acknowledgements

The grief process and the writing process are solitary work that cannot be done alone. Many people have helped the ideas in this book take shape and form, and become what you read today.

Thank you to Brooke Adams Law, Meg Dippel, Meghan Muldowney, Karinna Klocko, and everyone at Writing Brave Press for believing in me and in this book, and helping me to share my work with the world.

Thank you to my teachers and mentors. Dr. Janet Stauffer held my grief with me in the early days, and inspired me to use my voice in the therapy room and on the page. Diane Brandt, my spiritual mentor and friend, understood that sometimes grief had no words and walked with me through the full range of my emotions. Thank you to my coach and friend, Lisa, who helped me dream about how this book could help other grievers.

Thank you to Leah, Lou, Liz, Beth, Ramona, and Adam for accompanying me through the grief and the writing process. Your texts, phone calls, walks and talks, and shared meals helped nourish my heart, soul, and mind.

Thank you to my friends and early readers, Wendy, Russ, Teresa, Sherry, and Meghan. Your encouragement and feedback helped me continue to write one word after another.

Thank you to Polka Dot Power House and the Friday morning Woo-Woo Dots. Your energy and belief sustained me throughout the process and helped me dream that this book could indeed be possible.

Thank you to Sonya, the Parent & Sibling Loss Group, and the Surviving to Thriving Grief Group at the Pathways Center Hospice. There aren't words for the gift of having space to honestly share the complexity of the grief journey.

Finally, I offer my deepest gratitude to my family. My sisters Erin and Laura shared both the excitement and the bittersweetness of this book with me. My stepdaughter, Sophia, offered kindness and encouragement. I also want to thank my stepdaughter, Gabi, who read excerpts, helped me develop a marketing strategy, and encouraged me to pause when needed.

Finally, I thank my spouse, Joe, for being my first reader and my sounding board. More importantly, he always believed in this book and in me. I love you all.

www.ingramcontent.com/pod-product-compliance
Lightning Source LLC
Chambersburg PA
CBHW08075512026
46557CB00006B/1276